LOVING
DISCIPLINE
A to Z

ESTHER WRIGHT, M.A.

TEACHING FROM THE HEART

TEACHING FROM THE HEART
San Francisco, CA

ISBN 0-9642947-0-2

ABOUT THE AUTHOR

Esther Wright, M.A. has been both an elementary and secondary classroom teacher for many years. She worked primarily in special education in the San Francisco public schools and has been a teacher trainer at San Francisco State University.

Ms. Wright currently presents workshops throughout the country on issues related to discipline, inclusive education, teambuilding, and self-esteem.

Esther's previous book, *Good Morning Class-I Love You!* has been read and enjoyed by thousands of teachers throughout the world. She is also known for her *Successful Parenting* video series available through Greystone Educational Corporation.

If you are interested in scheduling a workshop or keynote presentation by Esther Wright, please call or write to:

TEACHING FROM THE HEART
P.O. BOX 460818
SAN FRANCISCO, CA 94146-6818
(415) 821-0447
OR
1-800-798-2686

This book is dedicated to my mother, Sophie Weiser Gray, who gave me the strength, confidence, and sense of responsiblity that allowed me to write this book.

Also, to my father, Hy Weiser, who taught me to love and respect all human beings.

And to my son, Stephen, who gave me the opportunity to pass on these gifts.

ACKNOWLEDGMENTS

There are many people to whom I am grateful and want to express my appreciation. First to all of the children I taught in Alhambra, Hayward, and San Francisco, California. And to the thousands of teachers I have worked with and learned from these last few years.

Also to my professional family ... the people who have contributed to my growth as an educator—Frank Siccone, Phil Harris, Jim Grant, Ted Harms, Brad Winch, Merrill Harmin and Sandi Redenbach. And to my fellow educators who share a commitment to transform discipline in education—Rick Curwin, Allen Mendler, and Linda Albert.

To all the people affiliated with Landmark Education Corporation and the Education Network for their commitment to make a difference in people's lives.

To my friend Bil Krehemker, who has provided me with large doses of love, support and encouragement. To my pals Sandi Redenbach and David Trousdale for their editing assistance. To my best friend, Dianne Maxon for her feedback and support and for being an exemplary teacher and parent.

And to Rich Ressman and the Isle of Marguerita for the high winds, sunshine and clouds ...

TABLE OF CONTENTS

To begin...

Schools should be places for learning,
laughing, and loving.
So teacher I ask you,

Did you *learn* today?
Did you *laugh* today?
Did you *love* today?

INTRODUCTION

T hese are tough times for teachers. We want our students to be happy and successful in school, however, during the last ten years *the challenges we face in the classroom have increased tenfold,* while in most schools, the resources available to us—as well as our morale, have decreased significantly.

Surveys conducted over the past few years have indicated that **discipline and student violence** are high on the list of teacher concerns.

- The National School Board Association tells us that every day approximately 135,000 guns are brought to school.

- Seventy-eight per cent of school districts reported student violence in the past year.

- Sixty-per cent of urban schools reported student assaults on teachers.

- Eighty-two per cent of America's school districts report that violence in the schools has increased significantly during the past five years.

These statistics are alarming and reflect a crisis in the schools that most teachers are unprepared to deal with. How did this happen?

The children of today are living in a society where disrespectful behavior is fashionable and violence is entertaining. Students are learning inappropriate attitudes and values from movies, T.V. and music lyrics that offend even the most liberal adult. Many of today's youth are entering our classrooms lacking values for respect, responsibility, and integrity. The resulting negative attitudes and behaviors make it increasingly difficult for us to remain loving and nurturing teachers.

Teachers are generally good people who want to do a good job in their classrooms. We have chosen a profession that provides us with the profound privilege of shaping young lives. We work very hard, are often underpaid, and rarely get the support and recognition we need to do our best work.

In spite of all this "gloom and doom", teachers must recognize and act on the opportunity we have to teach our students the important lessons they are not learning from our society-at-large.

- We must support and nurture the humanity of our students, while bringing out their best selves.

- We must allow them to observe and experience the value of being respectful and responsible.

- We must demonstrate that the *heart*, as well as the mind, can be used as a tool for confronting the challenges and obstacles that are integral to the living and learning process.

This book is about supporting *you* in being the caring, nurturing, and supportive teacher that students want and need in these difficult times. The ideas presented on these pages are meant to generate questions as well as answers about the "art of discipline" ... a topic that perplexes most of us, but one that this book hopes to address in a way that makes a difference in America's classrooms.

Thank you for being a teacher. May your journey through the years of this profession be one that is *joyful, loving, and empowering* for you and your students.

Always remember that your mission is to serve, support, and teach every child in your classroom.

♥ Teaching has always been a challenging and demanding profession, however, today's teacher is expected to teach larger numbers of students with a wider range of special needs. Few teachers feel prepared to teach these students effectively. This can cause frustration and feelings of inadequacy among even the most competent and committed teachers.

Although many of us would prefer to teach motivated, well-behaved children from stable families, we must face the realities of today's classroom. Some of our students have lived in poverty or unstable homes. Others come to us with learning difficulties or attention-deficit disorders. Many come to us with needs for attention and power that can cause a myriad of distractions in the classroom.

We can reach and teach all of these students, but it will require that we not let their behaviors and special needs distract us from our purpose for being in the classroom. We are not policemen or prison wardens. We are teachers who must find ways to contribute to the growth and development of students, both academically and socially. We must never underestimate the potential impact we have on the lives of our students.

Be a good role model.
You are *always* teaching.

♥ From the moment we step into a classroom we are teaching. Much of what we teach is not reflected in our lesson plans. There is an "invisible curriculum" being taught throughout the school day and it is as important as the facts and skills we teach our students.

Our students learn a great deal from observing how we relate to them as well as how we relate to other staff members in the school. They notice if we are responsible, respectful, and integrous. They can learn how to deal with disappointment, frustration, and anger from observing how we handle these emotions in the classroom.

Watch yourself and listen to yourself. What are you teaching your students about being responsible, kind and respectful human beings?

Communication skills are essential to good teaching. Communication is more than talking to students. It involves speaking *with* and listening *to* students with an open mind and an open heart.

Changing *your* attitudes and behaviors will often produce changes in student behavior.

♥ From time to time we need to remember that changing our attitudes, *(this student is **needy**, rather than bad)*, and changing our behaviors *(being **positive** rather than **punitive**)*, will assist us in being more effective when dealing with discipline issues in our classroom.

Our perceptions determine our reality. If we think a child is a bad person or an insoluble problem, our voice, body language, and actions will reflect those perceptions. In most cases, this results in students becoming more defiant and defensive in order to deal with our negativity. Students tend to be cooperative with people they trust and respect.

Pay attention to your perceptions. Change the ones that serve as obstacles to being creative, optimistic, and supportive towards your troubled students.

The classroom, like a fine orchestra of instruments, with various sounds and textures— awaits the great maestro to bring out the best of each instrument—while directing the lovely harmonies and melodies we call learning.

Develop relationships with your students that reflect caring and respect.

♥ Do everything you can to establish and maintain caring and respectful relationships with your students. Treat them as you would want to be treated. Unfortunately, this does not guarantee that they will always be respectful towards you. Many of these students have learned inappropriate ways of communicating their wants, needs, and feelings.

The big test occurs the first time a student speaks or acts disrespectfully to you. Comments such as "you're a boring teacher", or "this is a dumb assignment " get some teachers upset. Others will pretend not to hear these comments knowing they are used by students to get attention or power. Still others might respond by calmly saying, "We don't talk like that in this classroom. We are respectful and kind to everyone at all times".

The important thing is to *not* take student misbehavior personally. Disrespect is learned behavior and can be changed. The best way to change disrespectful behavior is by modeling respect and acknowledging students who are being respectful in the classroom.

Of course we too will have our "off days" when we find ourselves forgetting to model positive behaviors. When you catch yourself in this situation, apologize to your class, allowing them to see that you are human and make mistakes.

Your students will respect you for your honesty and courage. They will get the message that you respect them enough to acknowledge *your* vulnerabilities and humanity.

Encourage students to demonstrate their goodness throughout the school day.

♥ Every student has the potential to behave and contribute positively to the classroom. Teachers can provide experiences that bring out the best in students.

For example, have students create projects where they are required to offer service or support to people in the classroom, school, or community. Allow them to report on their contributory projects orally or in writing. Invite the people who were the recipients of their service to share what it was like for them. When students have experienced the joy of giving and receiving, it contributes to their self-esteem and brings out their positive nature.

We may not have control over the negative histories our students bring into the classroom, but we can provide them with opportunities to experience their goodness. This is truly a gift to students who have forgotten that they are inherently good people.

There are moments in my teaching when I make a connection with a student that is so profound, it almost moves me to tears. In that moment, I am very aware of why I chose to become a teacher.

Forgive yourself and your students for not always being perfect.

♥ What do classrooms and gardens have in common?

Take a few moments to look at a garden in your neighborhood. Notice the lovely and interesting array of plants and flowers. If you happen to see a rose bush, stop for a moment and look closely at the roses. Notice how some are in full bloom and appear perfect. Others are still in the budding stage. Still others are insect-ridden or blemished in some way. Nonetheless, the garden, in spite of blemished flowers, snails, gophers, and wilted leaves, is a lovely setting for a picnic or relaxing afternoon nap.

It could be said that our classrooms, like gardens, are not always perfect. It could also be said that what we think to be imperfect is simply the way things are as we go through our growth process...

Your classroom can be a more satisfying learning environment for you and your students if you are able to accept that neither you nor they are perfect. It is, in fact, our imperfections that make us unique and interesting. Think about it.

Teachers, in learning to accept their own humanity, will be better able to accept and honor the humanity of their students.

Give your students opportunities to experience their ownership and responsibility for the classroom.

♥ Many of us were taught in traditional, autocratic classrooms where being responsible meant being quiet, paying attention, and doing what we were told. Some teachers are still trying to impose a 1950's discipline system in today's classroom with little success. Our students must learn that they are **equally** responsible for the success of the classroom.

In order for students to learn this important lesson, teachers should provide them with opportunities to have input regarding the discipline systems and policies. Allow students to brainstorm rules or agreements that will support everyone's learning. Discuss the obvious obstacles created when rules or agreements are not honored. Come to consensus about which rules will most support the classroom or take the results of the brainstorming activity and choose the ones that you feel will most support student success.

Being involved in this way offers students a sense of pride and ownership for the classroom. Defiant and resistant behaviors will be reduced and students will be motivated to honor the rules and agreements they themselves have developed.

> "Since we have two ears and one mouth, we should listen twice as much as we talk."
> —Tom Lehrer

Help your students develop empathy and compassion for each other.

♥ A student's ability to be empathetic and compassionate enriches their relationship with others and contributes to a harmonious classroom.

Your classroom is a community of learners who come together to grow and succeed. Do they appreciate and support one another? If you have students with special physical, emotional, or academic needs, you have the opportunity to encourage empathy and compassion. Allow students to share how they feel about "being different" or not having as many friends as other children. Have your students read books or view films about differently abled people. Simulation activities where students have a chance to "walk in the shoes of another person" can also create empathetic attitudes among students.

In addition, students can learn empathy and compassion by observing *your* responses to troubled (or troubling) students. Take a moment to reflect on what your students are learning when you deal with discipline problems in your classroom.

Implement a positive, pro-active approach to managing your classroom.

♥ Being proactive requires thinking ahead and attempting to predict what systems and structures your students will need in order to be successful. These systems and structures can prevent problems before they begin. How we arrange desks, where we seat certain students, how we manage the distribution and collection of materials, how we transition activities, and how we provide support to students who require individual attention are issues we must consider **before** school begins and then manage as the school year progresses.

When a disruption occurs, there are many positive strategies that work. Some teachers ignore minor misbehaviors and find that they disappear without any intervention. Other teachers walk over and stand near the student, sometimes looking at them or gently touching their shoulder to get their attention. Some teachers use 3x5 cards that say, *"please get back on task"* or *"are you being a responsible learner?"* Often these actions work as well as calling out a student's name or implementing a punishment.

In some cases, you must add or modify a system or structure that will prevent the behavior from reoccurring, (e.g. changing seating, setting up a game or contract, engaging the student in an activity they enjoy).

If you find yourself constantly criticizing students, or if you find the same behaviors occurring day after day, you can be sure something needs to be changed or added. Determine whether changes are needed in the physical arrangement, the discipline system, or the instructional program.

Stop, look, and listen to what systems and structures your students seem to need. If your predictions turn out to be inaccurate, don't get discouraged. Experiment with new systems and structures until you discover the ones that work best for this group of students.

Just do what you know is the *right* thing for each child. Listen to your heart.

♥ Have you ever followed the advice of an expert or discipline program and found that things got worse?. The experts may be well-intentioned and knowledgeable, but **they are not in your classroom, or in your body, dealing with this particular child at this moment.**

Discipline is not a "paint by numbers" phenomenon. There are many variables that affect what goes on in a classroom. The wise teacher consults with the experts to consider a variety of options, but the most successful teachers are the ones who listen to their **hearts** as well as their minds when dealing with challenging students.

None of the experts or programs can guarantee that their recommendations will work for every child, but be assured that disciplining from a place of caring and love will have a much better chance of succeeding, regardless of which strategies you use with your students.

And finally, be sure that any strategy or system you employ is consistent with your style, your values, and your integrity.

> "You cannot put the same shoe on every foot."
> —Publious Syrus

Know thyself.
Know thy students.

♥ When a teacher finds him or herself frustrated, angry, or fearful in the classroom, it is important to reflect on the source of these feelings. More often than not, these emotions are caused by the myriad of unfulfilled expectations we have of ourselves and our students... (we *should* be able to teach and manage every child; they *should* be ready, able, and willing to learn and cooperate).

As teachers, we do the best we can with the information, support, and strategies available to us. The same is true of children. Getting to know our students may help us to better understand why they behave the way they do. Understanding their behavior will support us in choosing interventions that are more likely to succeed.

Try having lunch with the students that mystify you the most. Use this opportunity to get to know them in a more friendly and relaxed setting. Their behavior may improve and your perspective may change when you shift the context and remove the demands and expectations of the student/teacher relationship.

Love your students.
Love them more.
Love them even more.

♥ There are many ways we demonstrate our love of teaching—spending long hours after school developing the perfect lesson plan, using our own money to purchase classroom materials, tutoring students before or after school. The list goes on and on...

You and I know many teachers who go beyond the call of duty. We also know many students whose needs extend far beyond the curriculum Although we can't always be a surrogate parent or social worker for these students, we must make sure they know we care about them.

Teach from the heart. Discipline from the heart. That is by far the most effective way to reach your needy and troubled students.

I do my best work as a teacher when my heart is open. When my heart is closed, teaching often becomes a struggle.

Maintain respect and dignity in your relationships with students, especially when dealing with discipline.

♥ There are several discipline programs that encourage teachers to treat students with dignity and respect. *Discipline With Dignity* and *Cooperative Discipline* are two such programs that I highly recommend. (See Reading List)

This is an important commitment to make to your class, but one that is sometimes difficult to honor and maintain. Remember that **your** behavior sets the tone for **their** behavior. It has been my experience that sooner or later even the most hostile students will become my allies if I consistently treat them with respect. And yes, sometimes they tested me to determine if I was being "real" with them.

Teach your students to value respect by reading stories or sharing experiences that demonstrate the importance of being respected and treating others as you wish to be treated.

USA Today, March '94 had this to say about corporal punishment: "Spanking tells kids that it's OK to hit people if you don't like what they do. It's not a lesson our schools should be teaching."

Never forget the powerful opportunity you have to impact the self-esteem and self-concept of the students you teach.

♥ It has been said that self-esteem is a greater indicator of success than intelligence. Self-esteem is the reputation one has with oneself. A student who feels *capable, valued, and loved* is going to have a better chance of reaching their full potential.

Throughout the school day, teachers have many opportunities to provide students with esteeming experiences, not by giving easy "A's" or false praise, but by allowing students to feel accomplished and authentically validated.

Self-esteem is experienced naturally when one is successful in the face of risk and challenge. *Cooperative Discipline* tells us that when students feel **connected** to others, **capable** in the classroom, and given opportunities to **contribute,** they develop self-esteem.

Reflect on the people and circumstances that have contributed most to your self-esteem. Attempt to emulate those people and offer similar experiences to your students.

Organize your classroom so that students have support systems available when they face academic or behavioral challenges.

♥ By nature, any growing/learning process includes some degree of frustration, confusion, fear, or failure. When students don't have support systems they tend to act out or cause problems as a way of expressing their frustration or fear of failure. It is a wise and loving teacher who proactively sets up systems to assist students when they are dealing with these stressful experiences.

At the beginning of the year, have students analyze and discuss how learning occurs and the emotions or experiences that accompany many challenging learning processes. Have them make recommendations for support systems that will foster student success.

Peer tutors, mentors, cooperative learning, computers, and teacher/student conferencing are possible systems that can assist students when they are dealing with stressful situations in the classroom.

> "What corrupts communication? Anger, fear, prejudice, egotism, and envy."
> —Guy de Maupassant

Pretend that your students are there to teach you the "art of teaching." They are.

♥ Most teachers are well versed in the "science" of teaching and discipline. We have read the books, attended workshops, and paid close attention to what the experts have told us. However, the "art" of teaching and the "art" of discipline are learned in only one place ... the trenches we call our classroom.

It was John Holt who said, "Everything I learned about teaching, I learned from 'bad' kids". My experience has been similar—knowing that I have gained valuable insights and strategies from the inner city special education students I worked with for many years. They were "bored and battered" kids, rather than bad kids, and they had a difficult time conforming to a traditional classroom where worksheets and textbooks were the primary instructional tools. They resisted, acted out, and consistently let it be known that they needed a more relevant and experiential curriculum.

I suggest that you allow your unmotivated learners to be your guides to great teaching. This process will not always be a comfortable one. But if you are *patient* and *positive* with yourself and these students, you will turn into a creative and resourceful teacher and find that you have fewer discipline problems in your classroom.

"To be a teacher in the right sense is to be a learner. I am not a teacher, only a fellow student."

—Soren Kierkegaard

Quiet, calm, and positive discipline interventions are the most effective kind.

♥ When students test or defy our authority, our tendency is to call out their name, threaten them, or embarrass them in front of their peers. Although these reactions will get your students' attention, they will not contribute to having a loving and emotionally safe classroom environment.

Practice using a calm, quiet voice when dealing with discipline. Use proximity (stand next to the student) and have a private, rather than public interaction *focusing on the behavior you want* rather than focusing on the behavior you're attempting to change.

If you develop these habits when dealing with disruption, you will notice students having less need to defend themselves with sarcasm and you'll find yourself less often engaged in power struggles with defiant students.

From time to time, ponder the behaviors and characteristics of people you trust and admire. Be that kind of person for your students as often as possible.

*R*espond rather than *react* when disciplining your students.

♥ There is a big difference between **reacting** and **responding** when dealing with discipline. Reaction in this context is saying or doing something triggered by an emotion, usually frustration or anger.

Teachers who *respond* rather that react are more effective because they are not allowing student behavior to distract them from their commitment to support and teach their students.

Responsive teachers don't take student misbehavior personally. They are clear and confident about their role and act accordingly. They may respond to misbehavior with a question, a request, or with humor.

Responsive teachers know they are modeling and teaching at all times. They may sometimes feel anxious or upset, but they find healthy ways of dealing with their stress. They get the support and coaching they need. They maintain their physical and emotional well-being by eating well, getting sufficient sleep, and exercising regularly. They find time to relax after school and participate in enjoyable activities on week-ends. They live a well-balanced life which allows them to deal effectively with the stress and challenges of the classroom.

> "Everything educates, and some things educate more than others."
>
> —Harold Taylor

Speak to your students as if they are future Harvard scholars.

♥ We shape our students' sense of self through our communication and relationships with them. If we interact with them as if they are capable and trustworthy they will eventually live up to our expectations.

Dr. Asa Hilliard, a noted educator, recommends that teachers "look for the genius in *every* child." I have always believed that children become who we say they are. Marva Collins and Jaime Escalante have demonstrated that at-risk students can excel in school when provided with challenge, support, and encouragement. Henry Levin's Accelerated Schools Project has also produced impressive results with at-risk students throughout the country.

Don't look at a student's cum folder to determine who they are. Most of all, don't let misbehavior allow you to forget that your students have gifts and talents to be developed and contributed.

Be the teacher who helps each student find the key to their treasure chest of abilities.

Goethe said, "Treat people as if they were what they ought to be and you help them to become what they are capable of being."

Trust that your students want to be responsible, successful learners. Sometimes they forget.

♥ Have you dealt with students who don't seem to care if you threaten or punish them? Students who won't follow class rules or turn in their homework?

These are the students who frustrate us the most. If we want to reach these youngsters, we must never assume they are beyond help.

Many of these students have been turned off to school as a result of failure and other negative experiences. Often these students are hurting emotionally but disguise their pain with an, "I don't care" or "don't mess with me" attitude.

It is possible to rekindle the joy of learning in these students, but it will require insightful and sensitive teachers who can see beyond the facade of toughness and negativity.

Sometimes these students need "space", sometimes encouragement, sometimes an opportunity to communicate their frustration and anger without being judged.

Many of these students have lost hope in their ability to be successful in school. They may forget who they really are from time to time, but *we* must never forget if we are going to reach them and teach them.

Understand the age-appropriate *needs, fears, and values* of your students.

♥ Our students have a wide range of needs, fears, and values that can make successful learning and appropriate behavior a challenge for them. For example, students who have a *need* for attention and power will often get it by interrupting our teaching or by annoying other students in the classroom.

Students bring *fears* into our classroom. Fears of not having friends, fears related to school success, or fears associated with a family situation (divorce, illness, etc.) These fears will distract them and result in anxiety or stress that can also affect their behavior in the classroom.

A child who *values* play and socializing over working in a textbook is not a **bad** child. Students of all ages *need to play*.

We must consider student needs, fears, and values when planning our instructional program and developing our discipline systems. A loving classroom provides students with appropriate doses of attention, power, stability, and opportunities to work *and* play.

Value each child's unique expression of self, even if it doesn't fit your pictures of how students should behave.

♥ In addition to their needs, fears, and values, students enter our classrooms with temperaments and perspectives that are unique and varied.

Some students are shy, some outgoing, some very aggressive. Our students may come from worlds that look different from ours, thereby giving them opinions and points of view that are not only different, but may conflict with our own.

This diversity of perspective and expression can make for a colorful and interesting classroom where students learn to appreciate difference of opinion and points of view. This opportunity can only occur if the **teacher** values each student's self-expression and unique point of view, all the while encouraging students to be respectful and contributory when sharing their perspectives.

A student-teacher relationship in which a student is required to behave and think in ways that reflect the temperament and perspectives of the teacher is not an esteeming or empowering one.

Strive for developing relationships with your students where self-expression is valued and encouraged. The best learning occurs when we are open and they are open to all perspectives and points of view.

"Communication doesn't flow. Sometimes it leaks, spurts, and bubbles."

—Edgar Cayce

Welcome parents as partners. Treat them with respect, and realize they are trusting you with their most precious possession.

♥ We sometimes forget that most parents want the same things for their children that we want.

They want their children to reach their full potential, get along well with others, and be happy and successful in school and in life. If we have a sincere intention to engage parents as partners we must relate to them with these common commitments in mind. Parents who think they are being blamed for their child's problems will tend to get defensive and not show up to parent-teacher meetings or other meetings called to discuss their child's needs.

Rather than blaming parents, we must help them set goals and take the actions needed to support their child's success. We should make recommendations that we feel will make a difference. Parents who consistently stay away from school are frequently parents who have major personal problems, (marital, financial, health), or have had negative experiences with school personnel in the past.

If we treat parents with respect, instead of judging them, we will find them more willing to be our partners in their child's education.

X

Examine your purpose for being a teacher. Does it inspire you? If not, find something else to do with your life.

♥ From time to time, remind yourself why you chose to become a teacher. It is easy to lose our inspiration and enthusiasm after five or ten years.

I have always believed that **teaching is the most honorable of professions.** I also know that teaching is a terrible job if you are doing it for the wrong reasons.

Many of us have worked with teachers who are "waiting for retirement". The sad truth is that some of these teachers have already "retired", even though they show up for school every day. Some of them suffer from burn-out and have little or no energy left for teaching or managing behavior. I worry about them and I worry about the students assigned to their classrooms.

As professionals we must each do our part to reinspire these teachers or encourage them to find another career. Students deserve more than the mediocre education they will receive from people who no longer love teaching.

Yearn to be a *great* teacher. Then do whatever is necessary for you to achieve excellence in your classroom.

♥ Being a *great* teacher is a worthy endeavor. It is a challenge and opportunity available to each of us. But it requires what Jaime Escalante refers to as "ganas" ... a desire or hunger ... for being the best we can be.

Those of us who call ourselves educators must come to terms with where we are in the process of mastering our craft. Are we doing whatever we can to make good use of our talents? Are we willing to get whatever training or coaching we need to improve our weaknesses?

Being a great teacher doesn't mean being the "perfect" teacher, but some of us get lazy and develop habits that block our path to excellence. Excellence requires acknowledging where we currently are, and then taking whatever steps are needed to continue learning and growing.

How many hearts and minds did you open today?

Zealously offer support and unconditional love to those students who are the most difficult to reach. They need it the most.

♥ Most students, including your most disruptive ones, will eventually respond if you are *patient, positive, caring, and supportive*. There are some students, however, with pain so deep and scars so thick that they are unable to respond positively to your caring. Please do not let these students discourage you, and by all means **do not give up on them.**

Some of these students have developed psychological or emotional defenses to protect themselves from being hurt. Many of these youngsters have lost trust in adults. They may not be ready or able to open their hearts to your support. If you find you are not reaching them, perhaps a peer, a counselor, or another staff member will be more successful. In the meantime, let them be, and turn your attention to those students who are ready and able to be served by you.

In some cases it takes a long time for seeds of caring to cultivate, and sadly with some students you may never see the fruits of your labor. *Don't let these situations make you hard and uncaring.* Use these students as the impetus to be the most loving and supportive teacher you can be.

You will eventually end your career knowing you gave the best of yourself to every student. Some of the "tough" ones will unexpectedly come back years later thanking you and describing the difference you made in their lives. It is during those special moments, (with a lump in your throat and a tear in your eye), that you will be reminded that **great teaching and effective discipline** *come from the heart!*

BREAKING THE CYCLE OF FAILURE OF AT-RISK STUDENTS

Some of our students are living in circumstances, (such as poverty), that are not of their choosing and of which they have little or no control. Often these students come to school with negative attitudes and behaviors that sabotage their success. Teachers refer to these students as "at-risk" because they fail academically and/or socially.

In schools throughout the country, educators are attempting to discover how to break the cycle of failure that we see occurring in greater and greater numbers. We know that many of these at risk youngsters have academic potential, but their behaviors serve as obstacles to their success and frequently lead to their dropping out of school or getting into serious trouble with the law.

THE CYCLE:

- A child is born into poverty, dysfunctional family, or other negative circumstances.
  ⬇
- Child develops low self-esteem (no sense of value) ... also varying degrees of sadness, anger, and frustration.
  ⬇
- Child exhibits negative, defiant behaviors at home and school.
  ⬇
- Parents and teachers respond with negative and punitive reactions. (anger/punishment)
  ⬇
- Child's self-esteem further diminishes. Anger, frustration increases.
  ⬇
- Negative and defiant behaviors increase as student gets older.
  ⬇
- Behaviors become more destructive, perhaps even violent.
  ⬇

- Student drops out of school. May become involved with drugs or crime to pay for drugs.

  ↓

- Student reaches young adulthood continuing the cycle of poverty, or may be incarcerated for drug use or crimes related to drug use.

This cycle is commonly found in America's inner city public schools, and is unfortunately becoming more and more common in low income suburbs and rural communities. Although teachers cannot change the conditions that initially cause the self-esteem and behavior problems, there is much we can do to provide a safe, nurturing, and supportive school experience for these youngsters.

Creating classroom environments and relationships that nurture and esteem our at-risk students is an effective way to break the cycle of failure. We must build trusting and respectful relationships with these students from the very beginning of their school career. If we consider the causes of their disruptive behaviors, we will hopefully remain empathetic and sensitive to what these youngsters need and provide them with support rather than punishment ...

This is not to say that these students should get away with disrespectful or disruptive behaviors. They must learn to be responsible for their behavior and ultimately for their lives. But responsibility should not be associated with blame. It should be viewed as a tool for empowerment and freedom.

It is suggested, that consequences be implemented in a *supportive* manner, rather than in a punitive manner. Punitive consequences further damage the self-esteem of these students. Natural and logical consequences, when feasible, are the most effective way for students to see the connection between how they behave and how the world around them will be affected. This form of consequence provides them with an opportunity to develop awareness and responsibility for their actions.

In addition to learning to take responsibility for their actions, the at-risk student must be taught conflict resolution skills, effective communication skills, and problem-solving skills. Only then will they have the tools necessary to transcend the circumstances that so often lead to a life of poverty and despair.

DISCIPLINE—
PUNISHMENT OR
TEACHING?

Discipline problems are usually perceived as something that takes us away from what we think we should be teaching. Perhaps classroom discipline problems are actually a reminder that some students need something other than what teachers are providing.

Our job is to **teach** our students, yet so often in the heat of frustration and anger we **punish** students, which often damages the student-teacher relationship.

How often do we punish them without fully understanding *why* they do what they do?

How often do we pass up important opportunities to teach them the life skills they'll need to use the content we're hoping to teach them?

After many years of teaching, I am still asking questions. There is one thing I am very sure of however, **I did not come into teaching to punish other people's children.**

QUESTIONS FOR REFLECTION OR DISCUSSION:

1. WHAT IS MY PURPOSE IN BEING A TEACHER?

2. DO I HAVE THE RIGHT TO PUNISH OTHER PEOPLE'S CHILDREN?

3. DOES PUNISHMENT WORK MOST OF THE TIME?

4. HOW DOES PUNISHING STUDENTS AFFECT MY RELATIONSHIP WITH THEM?

5. IS PUNISHMENT THE MOST EFFECTIVE WAY TO IMPROVE BEHAVIOR?

6. WHAT AFFECT, IF ANY, DOES PUNISHMENT HAVE ON MY ABILITY TO TEACH MY STUDENTS?

ALTERNATIVES TO CONSIDER:

1. TEACH STUDENTS TO BE RESPONSIBLE BY GIVING THEM INPUT, CHOICES, AND LEADERSHIP OPPORTUNITIES IN THE CLASSROOM.

2. TEACH STUDENTS ALTERNATIVE BEHAVIORS FOR EXPRESSING AND RESOLVING THEIR ANGER, FEAR, AND FRUSTRATION.

3. TEACH STUDENTS THE RELATIONSHIP BETWEEN THEIR BEHAVIORS AND THE *NATURAL* CONSEQUENCES OF THEIR BEHAVIORS.

4. TEACH STUDENTS HOW TO RESOLVE CONFLICTS AND SOLVE PROBLEMS.

5. CREATE CLASSROOM COMMUNITIES WHERE STUDENTS SUPPORT EACH OTHER IN BEHAVING APPROPRIATELY AND SUCCEEDING ACADEMICALLY.

6. HAVE EVERY RESPONSE TO MISBEHAVIOR BE GENERATED OUT OF YOUR CARING, SUPPORT, AND COMMITMENT TO *TEACH* THIS STUDENT.

REACTIVE VS. RESPONSIVE DISCIPLINE

Discipline can cause major stress in a classroom for both the teacher and the students. Yet there are teachers who *respond effectively rather than react negatively* to disruption and misbehavior in the classroom.

THE REACTIVE TEACHER

- Is constantly calling out students' names, criticizing, threatening, yelling, and upset much of the time.

- Has expectations about his/her ability as a teacher that are not being met.

- Has expectations regarding the student(s) that are not being met.

- Is frustrated, disappointed, and angry because expectations are not being met.

- Feels overwhelmed, inadequate, and unsupported.

- Self-esteem suffers.

- Takes student misbehaviors personally.

THE RESPONSIVE TEACHER

- Ignores minor infractions.

- Uses proximity rather than calling out names.

- Is aware of how his/her behavior affects a classroom climate and student/teacher relationship.

- Is always modeling behavior he/she wants from students.

- Sometimes uses humor to dissolve tension or power struggles.

- Keeps students purposefully engaged and motivated.

- Expects students to have a variety of needs. Makes every effort to meet those needs, instead of expecting students to meet teacher's needs.

- Doesn't take student misbehavior personally.

CLASSROOM RULES, AGREEMENTS, AND PLEDGES

SETTING UP THE CLASSROOM ENVIRONMENT

At the beginning of the school year, (preferably the first day of school), have a discussion regarding the *purpose, goals, and expectations* of your classroom. The discussion will allow students to see what they can contribute and learn from their participation with you and each other.

During the discussion ask open-ended questions such as, "What do you want and need to be successful in this classroom?" or "What have you found are the obstacles to learning and success?" Place no judgments regarding the responses of students. This is an opportunity for all of you to get to know each other and begin developing a trusting and supportive relationship. Student responses can be listed on a chalkboard, chart, or overhead projector.

After students have had the opportunity to communicate what they want and need and what obstacles sabotage their success, the teacher should add his or her wants, needs, and obstacles to the list.

A second discussion should allow students an opportunity to brainstorm, discuss and prioritize rules, agreements, or a pledge, as a way of providing structure and support for having the classroom be an effective learning environment for everyone.

RULES

Rules are set up to clearly communicate the expectations and guidelines of classroom behavior. They are most effective when developed with student input. They should be limited to four or five that are specific, positive, and reflect the tone or mood the teacher wants to maintain throughout the year.

Example:
- *Be respectful and kind to everyone in this classroom.*
- *Do your best work.*
- *Come to class prepared to succeed. (materials, good attitude)*
- *Support others when they need it; let others support you.*

AGREEMENTS

Agreements are similar to rules, but are a verbal or written contract students make with each other and the teacher. There tends to be less resistance to agreements, because students don't feel they are being dominated or controlled by someone or something outside of themselves. Agreements allow students to experience a sense of responsibility and ownership for their behavior. Students can discuss or brainstorm agreements that would support everyone's success and then vote on the four or five they feel are important. The teacher may wish to speak on behalf of those agreements that will most benefit the classroom.

Example:
- *I agree to come to class on time.*
- *I agree to do my best work at all times.*
- *I agree to treat everyone with respect.*
- *I agree to support my teacher and peers so they can be successful.*

Students can make an oral agreement or sign a written contract. The issue of keeping or honoring one's word should be discussed as an issue of integrity and responsibility. Needless to say, some students will need to be reminded about their agreements. This should be done positively and respectfully by the teacher and a peer support team can be set up to assist students who are having difficulty keeping their agreements.

THE CLASSROOM PLEDGE

A classroom pledge can be developed by students on the first day of class, then posted and distributed to all students. The class should have the opportunity to discuss what a pledge is (a promise), and be encouraged to keep their word regarding the promises they make. Teachers can talk about the "Pledge of Allegiance" and what it represents. If the classroom pledge is developed by the students and represents what they want and need, it will have a good chance of supporting appropriate behaviors. The pledge can be read and discussed daily for the first week of school, and then read on Mondays of each week or when a refresher is needed throughout the school year. Secondary students may prefer to call this a "creed" and develop it as a personal guideline for their school or life success.

Example:

I PROMISE TO TREAT EVERYONE IN THIS CLASSROOM WITH RESPECT AND KINDNESS.

I PROMISE TO CONSIDER OTHER PEOPLE'S POINT OF VIEW.

I PROMISE TO PROVIDE SUPPORT TO MY TEACHER OR FELLOW STUDENTS WHEN NEEDED.

I PROMISE TO DO WHATEVER IS NECESSARY TO HAVE THIS CLASSROOM BE A SAFE AND SUCCESSFUL LEARNING ENVIRONMENT FOR MYSELF AND OTHERS

_____

SIGNED

LEARNING STYLES AND BEHAVIOR

Do you have students who seem to want to touch *everything* and *everybody* in the classroom? Or students who are always socializing instead of staying on task? How about the students who always want to know *why* they are being asked to do a particular assignment and never seem to answer an oral question directly, but prefer to tell you "stories" about the topic in question?

Do these students annoy you? Do you find yourself constantly nagging these students to get back on task? **Perhaps these students are "on task", but exhibiting a learning style that doesn't fit our pictures of on task behaviors.**

Teachers have been hearing about learning styles during the last few years, but mostly in regard to academics and instruction. Perhaps we must also consider how learning styles can affect classroom behavior.

Teacher observations and preliminary studies indicate that many of our at-risk students have similar learning styles. The dominant sensory modality of many of these students is **tactile-kinesthetic.** Although these students learn best through their bodies and feelings, most classrooms beyond kindergarten are primarily auditory and visual.

Educators have begun to investigate the possibility that there is also a *cultural* learning style that affects learning and behavior. It is believed that many of our Hispanic and African-American students, are **"relational learners"** ... that is, given the choice of learning from a book or a person, they will often choose a person. Could this explain why cooperative learning has maintained its popularity for many years and has proven itself to be an effective instructional format for at-risk students?

Studies also suggest that many at-risk students tend to be more **global-random** (right brained), than sequential-analytical (left-brained) learners, yet most classrooms after third grade are more structured, sequential, and require more left-brained abilities to succeed.

The student who wants to touch things and move around will get into trouble for not staying in their seat and completing their assignment.

The student who is bored with sequential or analytic activities will probably get into mischief, either by clowning around or socializing.

The relational learner will want to have friendly conversations with peers or with the teacher instead of completing a chalkboard or worksheet activity.

In short, these students will often be criticized and reprimanded for expressing their natural and dominant learning styles.

What could be more frustrating? Could this explain why so many students get turned off to school after the primary grades? Could this also be why a secondary student can be cooperative and well-behaved in their first period class, (where the teacher offers opportunities for classroom discussion and hands-on projects), and then become the class clown in second period, (with the teacher who primarily lectures and assigns reading and writing activities?)

Discipline problems rarely occur in a vacuum. They are often related to how effective we are in keeping students engaged in purposeful, motivating, and successful learning activities. The teacher who offers a variety of learning experiences and instructional formats will probably find students more cooperative and successful in the classroom. Having their learning style needs met, and having opportunities to be successful, will support these students in staying in school and getting the skills they need to be productive citizens.

A FOUR-STEP PROCESS FOR CHANGING BEHAVIOR

STEP ONE: REFLECTION

1. Observe student behavior with **objective** eyes and ears.

2. **When** does misbehavior occur most often? (Mondays, afternoons, transition periods)

3. **Where** does it occur most often? (at desk, on playground)

4. What **benefit** or payoff does the student get from this behavior? (attention/power)

5. What **circumstances** in this student's life could be a contributory factor? (divorce, poverty, academic failure)

6. Is there **a physical or neurological condition** that causes or contributes to this behavior? (check school records, speak to parents)

STEP TWO: COMMUNICATION

1. Set up a meeting with the student.

2. Ask friendly questions before giving advice or making requests. i.e. "How are things going for you in the classroom?", "How are things going with your family and friends?"

3. Ask the question, "What do you need to do your best work in this class?"

4. Ask the question, "Are you willing and able to honor the class rule or agreement regarding ...?" (If student is unwilling, find out why)

5. Ask the question, "What kind of support do you need?"

6. Set up follow-up meeting to discuss progress.

STEP THREE: SUPPORTIVE ACTION

1. Focus on changing **one** behavior at a time.

2. Begin by implementing whatever support student requested. (if feasible).

3. Make changes in seating, if appropriate. (less distraction, better models)

4. Modify instructional activities or time expectations, if appropriate.

5. Design contract or game to provide support and structure for behavior change.

6. Assign "buddy" or mentor for monitoring and support, if appropriate.

7. Engage parent support or counselor support, if needed.

STEP FOUR: FOLLOW UP

1. Meet with student to discuss progress.

2. Determine if additional supportive action is required.

3. Modify actions as needed.

4. Acknowledge willingness and effort of student to improve behavior.

5. Offer encouragement or incentives, as needed.

Note: Return to Step One and Step Two if supportive actions are not working effectively.

WHAT DOES THIS STUDENT NEED?

Use the following list as a menu, remembering that *different students respond to different interventions based on their needs and the causes of their behaviors:*

Does this student need ...

_____more success and validation?

_____opportunities to be a leader and to contribute?

_____more specific or clearer guidelines for behavior?

_____a behavior management contract?

_____a mentor or buddy?

_____an opportunity to communicate? (journal writing, drawing, counseling)

_____an opportunity to "let off steam?" (jogging, punching clay, kicking balls)

_____more rigorous consequences? (only after natural/logical ones have failed)

_____good role models?

_____more one-to-one attention? (aides, volunteers, peer tutors)

_____shorter assignments? (for students with short attention spans or cognitive delays)

_____more choices regarding assignments and classroom activities?

_____ parental support?

_____ more tangible rewards?

_____ a special quiet place?

_____ conflict resolution skills training?

Implement one or more of these supportive actions until you discover the one that is effective for this student. How you implement these actions is as important as choosing the right one. Remember to be calm, confident, and positive. Make sure the student experiences these actions as **support** rather than punishment.

DIFFERENT STUDENTS REQUIRE DIFFERENT KINDS OF SUPPORT

STUDENTS WITH DEFIANT TEMPERAMENTS

- Teacher must remain calm and confident when interacting with defiance.

- Do not get into power struggles or justify your point of view.

- Give them some choices and some opportunities to have it "their way."

- Consistently follow up on requests you make.

- Acknowledge them when they are following directions appropriately.

STUDENTS WHO DEMAND ATTENTION

- Greet them when they enter the classroom.

- Seat them near where you teach.

- Give them opportunities to work with other students.

- Check in with them several times during seatwork activities.

- Use their name in spelling sentences, math word problems, etc.

- Acknowledge them when they are on task.

- Try to ignore inappropriate attention-getting behaviors as much as possible.

STUDENTS WITH A LOT OF ENERGY

- Provide them with opportunities to move during class period.

- Have them run errands for you.

- Suggest they sign up for after school sports activities.

- Let them work with computers, manipulatives, or other interactive activities.

- Set up games and behavior modification systems (timers, etc.). that allow them to become more aware of and better able to control their need for movement.

STUDENTS WHO ACT DISRESPECTFULLY TO PEERS AND ADULTS

- Make sure you are always modeling respect when you speak to these students.

- Have them write or discuss how they like to be treated by others.

- Have the class write VIP letters to these students acknowledging them for their positive behaviors and attributes. (to improve self-concept)

- In elementary school, have student wear ribbon or sign that says, "I am a good friend" or "I have good manners."

- In secondary school, set up a *private* conference where you attempt to establish a friendly relationship with student.

- Make suggestions for alternative language, inflection, and ways of dealing with impatience, frustration, or anger.

STUDENTS WHO APPEAR UNMOTIVATED OR RELUCTANT TO LEARN

- Provide them with leadership opportunities.

- Find out what their interests and talents are. Assign activities related to their interests and talents.

- Pair them up with a "buddy" who is motivated and achieves academically.

- Give them choices regarding assignments.

- At the beginning, modify activities and timelines to ensure success.

- Offer peer tutoring to enhance student's confidence and success.

STUDENTS WHO FIGHT, ARGUE, AND BULLY

- Provide them with service opportunities. (peer tutoring, school projects)

- Give them opportunities to be monitors and leaders.

- Give them choices.

- Read stories or view videos that address appropriate ways of dealing with anger and frustration.

- Teach conflict resolution skills.

- Provide cooling off area and activities. (quiet music, journal writing)

- Provide opportunities for them to see a school counselor or psychologist.

RECOMMENDED READING

Albert, Linda, *Cooperative Discipline*, American Guidance Service, 1989

Bluestein, Jane, *21st Century Discipline*, Scholastic, Inc. 1988

Canfield, Jack and Siccone, Frank, *101 Ways to Build Student Self-Esteem and Responsibility*, Allyn & Bacon, 1993

Curwin, Richard, *Rediscovering Hope*, National Education Service, 1992

Curwin, Richard and Mendler, Allen, *Discipline With Dignity*, ASCD, 1988

Glasser, William, *Control Theory In The Classroom*, Harper & Row, 1986

Goens, George and Clover, Sharon, *Mastering School Reform*, Allyn & Bacon, 1991

Harmin, Merrill, *Strategies To Inspire Active Learning*, Inspiration Strategy Institute, Edwardsville, IL, 1994

Kreidler, William, *Creative Conflict Resolution*, Scott, Foresman & Co., 1984

Kuykendall, Crystal, *From Rage To Hope: Strategies For Reclaiming Black & Hispanic Students*, National Education Service, 1992

Lickona, Thomas, *Educating For Character*, Bantam Books, 1991

McCarney, Stephen, Wunderlich, Kathy, Bauer, Angela, *The Teacher's Resource Guide*, Hawthorne Educational Services, Colombia, MO, 1994

Mendler, Allen, *What Do I Do When?* National Educational Service, 1992

Nelson, Jane, *Positive Discipline*, Ballentine Books, 1987

Redenbach, Sandi, *Self-Esteem: The Necessary Ingredient For Success*, Esteem Seminar Programs and Publications, Davis, CA 1991

Reider, Barbara, *A Hooray Kind Of Kid!*, Sierra House Publishing, El Dorado Hills, Ca., 1988

Tobias, Cindy and Guild, Pat, *How to Use Your Learning Style To Be a Better Student*, The Teaching Advisory, Seattle, WA., 1986

Wright, Esther, *Good Morning Class—I Love You!*, Jalmar Press, Rolling Hills, CA, 1989

To: *The Teacher Reading This Book*

From: Esther Wright

Re: Feedback

Authors rarely get a chance to speak to their readers, so I have decided to take this opportunity to **thank you for choosing this book.** The teacher interested in a book with this title is the teacher I would want for my own child. So even though I don't know you personally, *I value and appreciate the work you do and the love you give to your students.*

Please feel free to send me any feedback that would contribute to my growth and development as an educator. If you have insights, strategies, or thought-provoking quotes, I would very much appreciate hearing from you. I also collect cartoons that deal humorously with the issue of discipline or teaching.

If this book has contributed to your work as a teacher, please take a moment or two to share your experience(s) with me. I would love to hear from you.

Please write to P.O. Box 460818 San Francisco, CA 94146.

Thanks so much.

And finally,

School is a place for learning, laughing, and loving.
So teacher, I ask you ...
How many of your students *learned* today?
How many of your students *laughed* today?
And how many hearts did you open?

ORDER FORM

LOVING DISCIPLINE AND TEACHING FROM THE HEART PRODUCTS AVAILABLE TO TEACHERS AND SCHOOLS

BOOKS:

QUANTITY   PRICE PLUS S/H

____ LOVING DISCIPLINE A TO Z $9.95+2.00 _____

____ GOOD MORNING CLASS—I LOVE YOU!   7.95+2.00 _____

____ GOOD MORNING CLASS—I LOVE YOU!   1.50+.50 _____
        BUTTON

AUDIO TAPES:

____ BREAKING THE CYCLE OF FAILURE   8.00+1.00 _____
        BY BUILDING SELF-ESTEEM

____ LOVING DISCIPLINE   8.00+1.00 _____

VIDEO TAPES:

SUCCESSFUL PARENTING *(3 part series)*

____ Full Set (Featuring Esther Wright)   239.00+4.00 _____

Also Sold Individually - ($85+1.50 S/H)   _____

____ BEING THE BEST PARENT YOU CAN BE

____ BUILDING SELF-ESTEEM IN YOUR
        CHILDREN

____ DISCIPLINE THAT EMPOWERS
        CHILDREN

California residents: Please add sales tax   TOTAL ENCLOSED _____

Make Check Payable To: **TEACHING FROM THE HEART**
Mail To: **P.O. BOX 460818 SAN FRANCISCO, CA 94146**
Or Call: **1-800-798-2686**   (Purchase Orders Accepted)

NAME_____

ADDRESS_____
            Street or P.O. Box   City   State   Zip